content

the color issue

▶ welcome to Modblock

We are so thrilled to introduce our first edition of Modblock. This is something we have wanted to do for a very long time. Our philosophy has always been that quilting should be fun, that there are no quilt police, and that a mistake is really just a new idea waiting to be developed!

We feel the Modern movement fits in perfectly with our thinking. Modern quilts have sparked our desire to learn and try new techniques, to play with shapes, try new colors, and break down the rules and barriers of traditional quilting. These types of patterns are perfect for beginners who are ready to break into the world of quilting. They are also fun for the more seasoned quilter who is ready to try something new. There is a new-found freedom that you feel when making a modern quilt. You can follow the pattern or break free and choose your own design path. There are no rules, just great ideas to help you get started! In this edition we will discuss color theory, improvisational piecing, traditional paper piecing, quilt-as-you-go, and the use of traditional quilting tools in unexpected ways. It is our goal to get you excited about trying new things and taking some quilting risks. We think the results will amaze and inspire you. We are so excited to share this with you and hope you enjoy this edition of Modblock. Let's go make cool stuff together!

—Jenny and the MSQC Team

▶ Alexia Abegg

Founding designer for Cotton + Steel
www.cottonandsteelfabrics.com

▶ Amy Ellis

Author & fabric designer for Moda Fabrics
www.amyscreativeside.com

▶ Vanessa Vargas Wilson

Host of The Crafty Gemini youtube channel
www.youtube.com/thecraftygemini

▶ Lisa Hirsch

Teacher & Kansas City Modern Quilt Guild member
MSQC modern quilt challenge winner

▶ Molli Sparkles

Blogger and award-winning quilt designer
www.mollisparkles.com

▶ Shea Henderson

Author, blogger & quilt designer
www.emptybobbinsewing.com

▶ Natalie Earnheart

*Chief editor and contributing designer
for Modblock & Block magazine
www.missouriquiltco.com*

▶ Jenny Doan

*MSQC Quilting Maven and host of
our youtube channel
www.missouriquiltco.com*

thank you.

We are especially grateful to our wonderful contributors. These fabulous people

have helped shape and fill this special issue of Modblock with gorgeous quilts and

informative articles. We love the sense of family and community that we feel from

the amazing and talented people in the quilting industry. They have been a pleasure

to work with and we have learned so much along the way.

Where do you find color inspiration?

The simple truth is "color inspiration" may be more a process of becoming "color aware." We are surrounded every day by color and tend to gravitate toward colors we like. We fill our favorite spaces with these colors, we dress in these colors, and we generally like

things created in these colors. They have a strong effect on our emotions, perhaps because these colors have brought us comfort at some point in our childhood or remind us of a place we love. These colors can affect our mood positively.

As you can imagine, this makes choosing colors a very personal exercise. One person's love for chartreuse is another's nightmare. It's important to start understanding your own likes and dislikes so you can begin to pick and combine color palettes that inspire you.

So where do we start? It's easy. Inspiration is everywhere. Look around you. Search your home. Gaze upon your closet of clothes. Peruse old pictures.

Visit your favorite locales. Start to create a mood board of color in your mind. Your colors of choice will quickly manifest themselves and you'll soon discover that color inspiration can come from everything, from a painting you love to even your favorite store or coffee shop. Once you have the source, start looking to it for the colors that jump out at you.

At this point, a fun approach involves a trip to the paint store and picking up a bunch of color swatches you love. Take them home and start pairing them together. Pull colors from your items of inspiration that you like and see if they make a good group. (I could seriously do this for hours.) Once you have a combination of 4-6 colors that you feel works well together there are a few things to consider.

gathering what you like

Pull together the things you love. Old photos, books or postcards from a trip, acorns from your favorite path, your grandma's teacup. All these things can come together to help you form ideas about the colors that inspire you.

pulling together your inspiration

Sorting things into groups can help you find your focus. Pick a color combination you like then pull from your inspiration to create a mood board. Pulling in textures, or patterned shapes will help give you ideas on what to create, what shapes you want to include or textures to use. As you work on your project you can reference back to these ideas to either refocus or as a sounding board for other projects.

▶ the color wheel

I'm sure you grew up knowing the 3 main primary colors: red, yellow, and blue. The color wheel takes these colors and breaks them down into three categories based on hue: primary, secondary, and tertiary. Let's take a closer look at the first two on the color wheel.

Primary Colors - These are the three pigments that are mixed to create every other color. All other colors are formed from these three. They are the building blocks of color!

Secondary Colors - These are colors formed from mixing the primary colors in different combinations (ie: blue + yellow = green).

▶ color value

Now that we have a general idea of how the color wheel works, there are a few other things to consider: How do colors respond to one another? For example, let's take red and contrast it with different color backgrounds. Red appears brighter against a black background and somewhat duller against a white background. In contrast, the red appears dulled when paired with orange, and brilliant when set against blue. In quilting we are constantly juxtaposing fabrics of different colors. How do those colors play off each other and are these the effects we are trying to achieve?

This is where the color wheel comes in handy. You can use the color wheel to choose lower contrasting colors or higher contrasting colors depending on their placement on the wheel. Higher contrast comes when you combine colors that fall across from each other. These are called complementary colors. Examples are orange and purple, green and red, and blue and yellow. Colors located close together on a color wheel are often used to create monochromatic color palettes.

Depending on your choice of color and the pattern you choose, you'll want to consider the following:

- Does the pattern require high contrast areas or will it work with a monochromatic look?

- Do your color choices blend?

- Where do you want the focus of the quilt to be—on the design, or on the color?

- Do you want one or several colors to stand out? If so, make sure the eye follows those color choices by adding contrast and repeating them evenly throughout the quilt.

The use of monochromatic and complementary color is about guiding the eye. Adding contrast and employing repetition evenly throughout the quilt will bring about a successful project.

▶ **value & tone**

Another important aspect to consider is overall value in color placement. Positioning two colors of the same hue or value together results in another interesting outcome that is very important to overall quilt design. For example, even though blue and purple are clearly different colors, they read as the same value. Do you want to have more contrast in your color group or less contrast? Colors of the same hue or value will give you less contrast and blend together for a more homogenous look. Likewise, pairing colors with higher contrast ratios will yield more pop and separation.

▸ Watch your tone

article by Molli Sparkles

As a teenager, my Grandma Sparkles used to always say to me, "Watch your tone, young man!" This was usually followed by a pointed finger and stern stare. I'll admit, I could sometimes be too smart, scratch that, too much of a smart alec for my own good. Fortunately, my mouth and I lived to tell the tales of my youth. But now, I think back to that phrase, and how it so serendipitously applies to quilting. So, what is tone? Forgetting for a moment the audible connotations of the word, tone has a huge role in the world of color. A tone is made when you add either black or white to any color on the color wheel. The reason to think about the addition of black or white separately, rather than singularly, as gray, is so they can be added in different amounts to achieve different effects. Most people are already rockin' out with tone, and they don't even know it!

Let's pause here and give some real life examples before anyone's bobbin gets wound up too tightly. Remember quilting in the nineties? It was nothing but hardcore tone! Think about all those dusty pinks and country blues that were mixed together in hearts and nine patches and Sun Bonnet Sues. (You aren't seriously still making those, are you?) Or go back a bit earlier to the marvels of sea foam green and peach fan quilts embellished with cream lace. Now, there was some tone! Yes, I know it hurts—I'm still trying to erase those images from my brain, too, but there's no denying the past! Tone didn't just exist in days gone by. Pantone's color of the year for 2014, Radiant Orchid, is simply red-violet with a touch of black and a heap of white. Tone is alive and well, folks, alive and well!

There is a reason color tones have been so popular through the years—they work so well together. They all have gray in common so they have an easy level of cohesion. Also, most of what we see

in the real world is a tone of some variety. This means there is a level of "comfortability" when we use them in the color schemes of our quilts. Now, who here doesn't want their quilt to be comfortable? I thought so.

I can see these wheels now spinning around in your head. You understand what tone is, and why you might want to use it, but the all important question is, "How do I use it effectively?" You are right to be a bit confounded by that one. I'm sure you've heard the cliche: variety is the spice of life. Well, it applies to tone as well. Mix them up and shake them down to achieve the greatest amount of interest in your quilt's color scheme. A color palette employing the same level of tone throughout runs the risk of feeling flat, which some might even call, monotone. (The prefix "mono-" means one, or singular). Instead, try juxtaposing a medium blue like cobalt, with the lighter tones of coral, lavenders, green, daffodil with a smoldering burgundy! You'll quickly see that colors start to come alive and vibrate off each other when you purposefully contrast their tones.

That's not to say this is the end-all and be-all of tone. Look up in the sky on a rainy day and you're likely to see a rainbow sparkling through the clouds. But this translucent light often appears monotone because of the grey clouds behind it and the atmospheric conditions of the sky you're looking through to see it. Who doesn't love a rainbow, right, even if it is monotone?! While monotone can produce a sense of flatness in your color palette, its regularity could also produce a sense of unity. By being aware of what is happening with the tones you decide to use, you can alter them to produce your own desired effects.

Finally, don't think for one split of a hot second that tones are dull or boring. Helloooooo, jewel tones! Sapphire, emerald, ruby, amethyst, citrine, oh my goodness, dip me in and shake me all about! Diamonds may be a girl's best friend, but these colors are a quilter's sexy love affair! Ow! These colors may be the easiest place to start exploring tone because they tantalize the eyes with sensations of luxury. You can mix and match them with ease, and you'll often find one or more of them featured in many designer fabric collections. (Allison Glass,

tone it up

Whether it's bright color tones of hot pink, red, blue or purple, these colors will be sure to delight the eye and add some bang to your quilting buck.

blend in or stand out?

Color value is a term that refers to how light or dark a color is when placed next to another color. Color value is every bit as important as color itself, because it helps quilters decide how to arrange patches of fabric to make them either blend or contrast with each other, and it's those arrangements that create a design. Change the color value/contrast of fabrics in your quilt blocks and you'll see a difference in the quilt's layout.

Anna Maria Horner and Zandra Rhodes spring to mind). So if you're still a bit scared of playing with tone remember: Everyone looks good dripping in jewels, so luxe it up!

Thankfully, Grandma Sparkles kept that bar of soap handy as she reminded me to watch my tone. It's led me to keep a fresh eye on it throughout my quilting career and a willingness to clean it up when needed. So start exploring the full range of tonal possibilities in your own quilts because you might just surprise yourself with some creative new color combinations. Whatever you decide, just don't let anyone tell you to tone it down!

all photos for this article contributed by Molli Sparkles

Quilting a quilt
which method works best for you?

Plenty of quilters will admit they have an unfinished stack of quilt tops laying around. I am also guilty of this. The actual quilting process can be rather daunting, can't it? Maybe you've pieced a quilt top, but haven't mastered the next step. Or you've quilted many times before and are interested in trying something new.

There are basically 4 different options to consider after you have answered a few questions at the onset. Which option you choose may be influenced by how much time you have to finish the quilt, whether you want to learn a new skill, if you want to hand the job over to someone else, how much money you want to spend or how many hurdles are involved.

Are you willing to spend money to have the quilt finished for you? If yes, you will need to plan around your longarm quilter's schedule.

Does the quilt need to be done ASAP? If so, your options are tying the quilt or machine quilting yourself, unless your longarmer can fit you in. Tying is quick and easy, but may not be the look you are trying to achieve. Quilting on your own machine involves making design choices and the ability to execute. A simple jump-off point may be to quilt by stitching-in-the-ditch.

Do you have both time and desire to learn something new? This may be the perfect opportunity to stretch yourself and try quilting by hand, or maybe free motion machine quilting is just the ticket. There are many facets of quilting you can master through classes, books, videos, your local quilt shop, or even a family member may be one of the resources you tap. Bottom line, choose a method that works best for you and get it quilted!

longarm quilting

Longarm quilting means investing in your own machine or finding someone who owns one to offer their services. Plus, if mastering the motor skills seems too much, there is the option of purchasing a computerized longarm machine that may suit you perfectly. There are endless design possibilities to pick from. The right design for your quilt can add depth and texture to your project. The more quilts you do the more you'll learn what styles and looks work best.

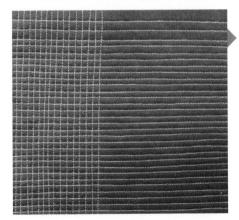

hand quilting

Quilting by hand is the most time-consuming technique, although it can render a very pretty and creative effect. The range of ideas can go from perfectly simple to very complicated. The use of colored embroidery thread can also add a beautiful effect. Whether using a straight stitch or creating an elaborate scene or decorative look, this technique is for the sewist that enjoys using her hands. A hoop or frame is required for this technique. It is perfect for smaller quilts or a special, homemade look.

machine quiliting

Quilted lines sewn at specific widths are often used by contemporary quilters. Straight line quilting creates a modern feel, and those lines contrast especially well with quilts that are full of curves and movement. Lines can be sewn in many directions! Vertical, horizontal, diagonal, crosshatch and diamonds are just a few ideas. These lines can be marked beforehand with chalk, fabric markers, painting tape, or a Hera marker. If you don't like marking up your quilts, a metal guide from your machine can be used.

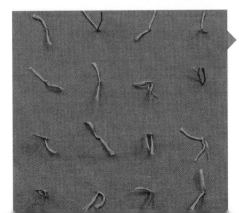

tying a quilt

Another technique is tying. Rather than sewing through the quilt sandwich, individual yarn or thread ties are used to secure all three layers together, usually three to four inches apart. This is a great activity to do with a group of friends or in a quilting bee and can go quickly the more hands you have to help. Depending on the size of the quilt you'll either need a frame or hoop to keep the quilt sandwich taut.

broken bars
shea henderson

The Broken Bars pattern is a terrific project for beginners and experienced quilters alike! It's a great start to improvisational piecing.

Say goodbye to fabric cutting lists, matching points and nesting seams, and experience quilting freedom. Once the pieces are cut, just toss them all in a bag and start sewing. It won't matter if you have two pieces that are the same size or color. Nothing has to be perfect, just trim your finished blocks to the same size and sew them all together.

One of my favorite things about this quilt is the illusion you can create by lining up some of the same fabrics. When you do this, the lines between blocks seem to disappear and this simple quilt looks a lot more difficult.

Have fun with this one! Play with color and prints, try a monochromatic color scheme, or go scrappy. This quilt is equally impressive whether prints or solid fabrics are used. The colors just seem to come alive. The options are as limitless as your imagination.

random can be liberating

How many times have you tried to sew a
"random" quilt just to end up with two of the
same fabrics together? Well with the Broken
Bars quilt you don't need to worry. Even if it
does happen, and it probably will, it will be
a happy mistake. The illusion of two of the
same fabrics together will create a larger
looking piece of the block and give
it a wonderful effect. Quilt police be gone!

solids vs. print

Whether you prefer solids or prints, this quilt is perfect for both. Using prints gives it a fun scrappy feel; using solids, a modern sophistication. You really can't go wrong, whatever your preference you'll be pleased with the results.

▶ supply list

makes a 67½" X 91" quilt

QUILT TOP
- (1) 22-24 fat quarter bundle

BINDING
- ¾ yd coordinating fabric

BACKING
- 5½ yds coordinating fabric

SAMPLE QUILT
- **Shaman** by Parson Gray for
  Free Spirit (warm colorway)

- **Patchwork City** by Elizabeth Hartman
  for Robert Kaufman (cool colorway)

▶ *visit msqc.co/modblock for tutorials*
& info on how to make this quilt.

1 cut

Remove the selvage from each fat quarter (FQ) and square up the fabric. Cut the FQ in half to make (2) rectangles about 18" x 10½." **1A** Before cutting make sure you are dividing the 21" side into 2 and that the ruler is perpendicular to the parallel edges. It's important to keep your cuts straight.

Next, subcut each rectangle into 10½" long strips x 2"-4" widths. These will be random widths but straight cuts. You will get approximately 6-8 strips per rectangle. Pay close attention that you are cutting along the 18" width. **1B**

2 sew

Let the fun begin! Throw all the strips into a bag or basket. Mix them up. The idea is not to overthink the color placement. But do avoid sewing two of the exact same strips together.

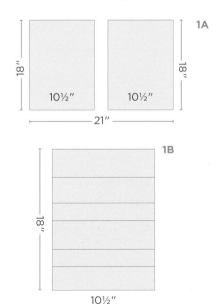

Grab 2 different strips and sew them RST (right sides together) along their 10½" lengths. Grab another strip and add it to create a column. Continue in this fashion until the column of strips measures at least 23." Press all the seams in the same direction. *(See the tip on how to avoid arcing.)* Square up the block to 10" x 23." Start a new one. Make 28 total. **2A**

3 layout

Arrange the blocks into a 7 x 4 setting. Sew blocks side-to-side across to make rows. **3A** Press seams to one side in rows 1 & 3; to the opposite side in rows 2 & 4.

Sew the four rows together. Nest the seams as you go. Press the horizontal seams down.

Quilt Center Size: 67" x 90½"

4 quilt & bind

Layer quilt top on batting and backing and quilt the way you like. Square up all raw edges.

Cut (9) 2½" strips from binding fabric to finish. For greater detail on finishing, check out the MSQC video tutorials. *See Supply List.*

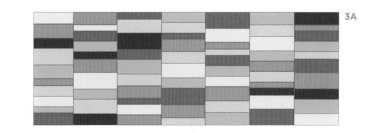

▶ **TIP** *Avoid arcing the block's strips when pressing. Have a hot iron on cotton setting with steam to press the seams. Set the seam first by pressing it just the way you sewed it, wrong side facing you. Then lift the top layer up 90° to the bottom layer and use the tip of the iron to run along the inside corner of the "L" shape. Avoid pushing or stretching the fabric. Allow the heat and weight of the iron to do the work for you. Now let go of the top layer and press the seam into its final position.*

1 Square up and cut the fat quarter. See Step 1.

2 Cut strips randomly ranging in size from 2"-4." See Step 1.

3 Sew random strips together along their 10½" side. Step 2.

4 Continue adding strip after strip.

5 Build a column of strips slightly longer than 23." Step 2.

6 Square up the column to 10" x 23." Make 28 blocks.

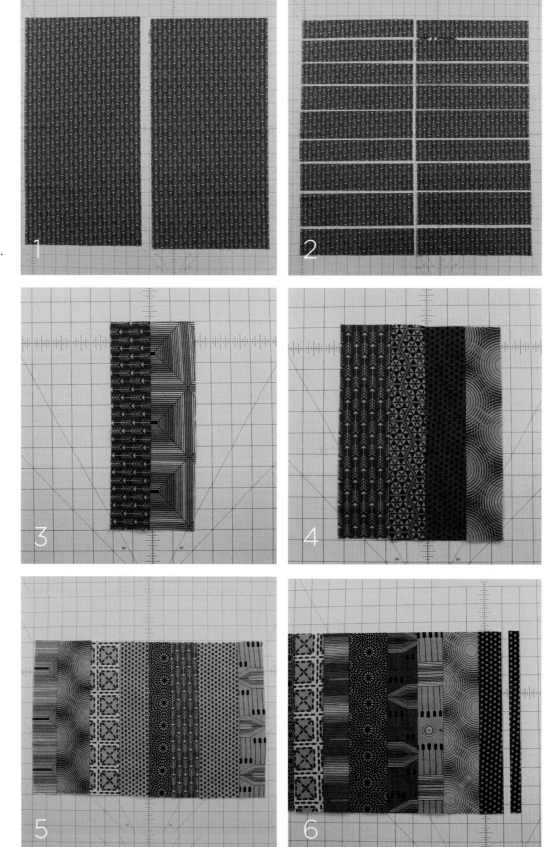

river log cabin
amy ellis

Have you ever seen an artist's painting that plays tricks on your eyes? These effects can make your brain think something is real even though you know it's not, like a door painted ajar that invites you to walk through it, or an apple sitting on a table that looks so real it begs to be eaten.

This artistic style that has been employed since ancient times is called trompe l'oeil meaning "trick of the eye" in French. The same effect can be created with all types of media. Fabric, of course, is our favorite.

Amy plays a trick on our eyes by stacking 2½" and 1½" strips to build a non-traditional log cabin block. By doing so, she creates a visual circle out of a square. It's the same traditional block we all know, but, with a new twist on the old favorite, a new block is born. Even though these are strips and squares, our eye fills in the gaps to create a wonderful effect of lost-and-found edges. Stepping back, the eye follows the background as it swirls around the circles like a river running past a log cabin.

▶ fabric makes the magic happen

Make a beautiful graphic statement with this pattern by using solid fabrics and bold colors. Or soften it for a more sophisticated and subtle effect by using Amy's fabric line Modern Neutrals by Moda Fabrics. No matter your preference, this pattern is sure to please. It has so many fun possibilities!

steady as she goes!

The key to a straight log cabin block is consistency. Keep your seam allowance a consistent quarter inch throughout. If you are pulling or trimming to make each piece fit, you'll be changing the size of the block and, each piece added after that will need trimming or pulling. Amy's design using a combination of thicker and thinner strips creates a log cabin block more quickly and with it, less chance for error!

▸ supply list

makes a 65" X 81" quilt

QUILT TOP
- (2) 2½" WOF print rolls
- 1¾ yds background solid OR (1)
  1½" WOF roll background solid

BINDING
- ¾ yd coordinating fabric

BACKING
- 5 yds OR 2 yds 90" wide

SAMPLE QUILT
- **Modern Neutrals** by Amy Ellis
  for Moda Fabrics

- **Bella Solids Eggshell** (281)
  by Moda Fabrics

▸ *visit msqc.co/modblock for tutorials
& info on how to make this quilt.*

1 cut & select

From all 2½" print WOF strips cut 5 segments from each measuring: 8½," 6½," 5½," 3½" & 2½"

From the background solid fabric cut (40) 1½" WOF strips. From each strip cut 2 each of 6½," 5½," 3½" & 2½" segments. **1A**

Total: 80 of each size; print & solid

2 build log cabin

The log cabin block is constructed by adding segments around a center. Here, 2 narrow segments are added to the center 2½" square followed by 2 wider strips. Chain piecing will speed up this process. Start with center squares and 1½" x 2½" rectangles. Feed a square and rectangle RST through the sewing machine with a ¼" seam. Continue sewing off the fabric a few stitches and feed the next pair through the machine and so on. Snip threads to separate blocks. Press away from the center for this block. Make 80.

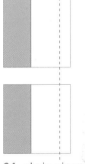

2A chain piece the same seam for all blocks

Each subsequent segment will cross the seam just sewn in a counterclockwise direction. Add to the center as follows:

1) 2½ x 1½ solid
2) 3½ x 1½ solid
3) 3½ x 2½ print
4) 5½ x 2½ print
5) 5½ x 1½ solid
6) 6½ x 1½ solid
7) 6½ x 2½ print
8) 8½ x 2½ print

Block size: 8½" x 8½"

3 arrange

Lay out the log cabin blocks in an 8 x 10 grid in the following manner: Two log cabin blocks are paired back-to-back so the print fabrics appear to form a half-circle. These half-circles alternate between facing up or facing down. **3A & B** Four half-circle pairs make a row. **3C**

Row 1: down, up, down, up
Row 2: up, down, up, down

Continue alternating rows 1 & 2 for a total of 10 rows. The final layout will reveal full circles in staggered columns on a background of white. Some columns consist entirely of full circles; others will begin and/or end with half-circles. **3D**

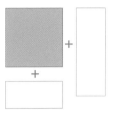

2B add a 2½" narrow segment to the center; then a 3½" narrow segment;

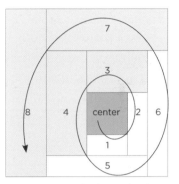

2C construct the log cabin in a circular sequence; 2½" segments are shown in light blue representing prints; 1½" segments are solid white

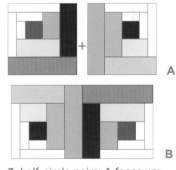

3 half-circle pairs: **A** faces up; **B** faces down

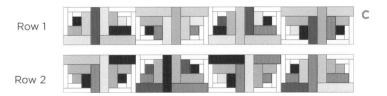

Row 1

Row 2

1 Begin with a print square and the shortest 1½" segment. Chain piecing will make quick work of building your log cabins blocks. Step 2.

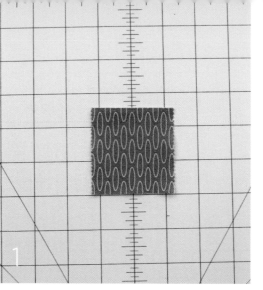

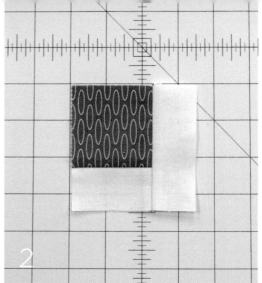

2 Add the next longer 1½" segment. You are moving counterclockwise around the center and crossing the seam that was just sewn. Step 2.

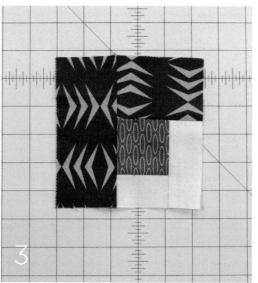

3 Next repeat the same counterclockwise direction but with 2½" strips. See the list in Step 2.

4 Now add (2) of the final 1½" strips.

5 After adding the final 2½" segments, you can see how the center appears to be surrounded by the wider strips on 2 sides. This will build the illusion of a circle when the blocks come together. Block size is 8½" square.

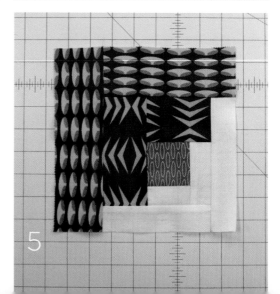

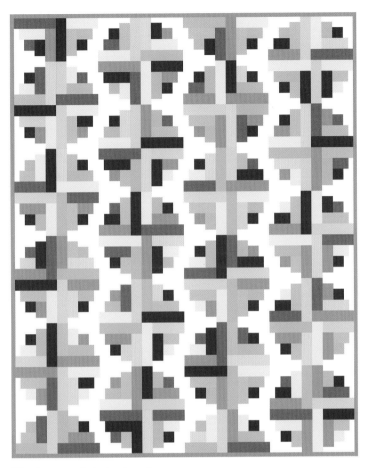

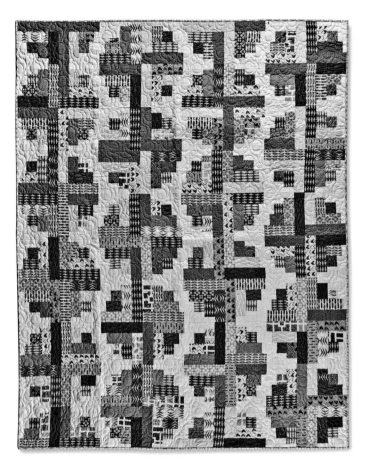

3D staggered circles in columns

4 sew it together

Begin by sewing blocks together across in rows; then rows together to complete the quilt top. Press all seams in even rows to one side; in odd rows to the opposite side. This will make nesting seams easy when sewing rows to each other.

Quilt Center Size: 64½" x 80½"

5 quilt & bind

Layer quilt top on batting and backing and quilt the way you like. Square up all raw edges.

Cut (8) 2¼" strips from binding fabric to finish. For greater detail on finishing, check out the MSQC video tutorials. *See Supply List.*

dapper dan
natalie earnheart

Baby Quilts are so much fun to make. They are quick, easy, and often a great place to try a new technique or block you've been eyeing. They are also a great way to practice your skills or challenge yourself to play with color or layout.

We decided to use the MSQC tumbler template and play with the negative space on this quilt. It made the job so easy and we love how the seams nested so well with each other to create this unique pattern.

To artists, the term 'negative space' refers to the area surrounding the subject of an image. In the quilting world, we often create negative space by adding sashing or a border or setting the block askew in a unique way.

Playing with negative space is a great thing to do with smaller quilts because you can test out concepts in a smaller workspace, thus requiring less effort. Try laying out your blocks on some extra background fabric or just use tape to mark off the boundaries of your desired quilt size. Place individual blocks around the space until you find a design that you like. It's helpful to take a picture of your layout along each stage so you can try different patterns without having to remember what you did. You might find you like several designs. Just save your extra ideas for your next project.

negative space is a positive thing

In this tumbler quilt, notice how negative space helps define composition as well as create movement. Imagine how the areas around the "bowties" might look if the fabric were patterned. Use of the white background gives this quilt an abstract quality while also allowing the eye to rest.

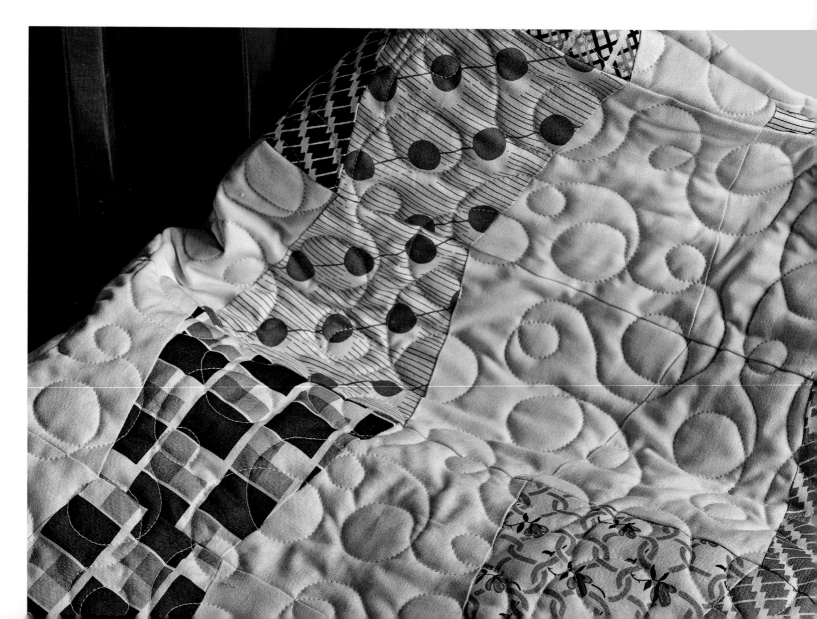

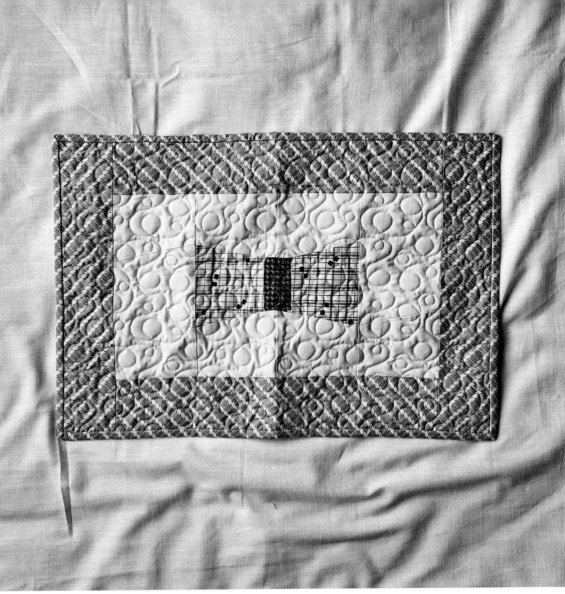

experimenting doesn't have to be scary

If you're not up for a baby quilt, try experimenting with a wall hanging or mini quilt. These can be just as fun and easy. Try changing the scale of your block to miniature size or play with different colors or fabric options to create a whole new look.

▸ supply list

makes a 46" X 56½" quilt
AND a 24" X 16½" pillow

QUILT TOP
- 2 packs 5" solid squares
- 1 pack 5" print squares
- ¾ yd outer border fabric

BINDING
- ½ yd coordinating fabric

BACKING
- 3 yds coordinating fabric

ADDITIONAL MATERIALS
- MSQC 5" Tumbler Shape

PILLOW TOP
- (10) 5" solid leftover squares
- (2) 5" print leftover squares
- ½ yd muslin
- 2" x 3" contrasting scrap
- fiberfill stuffing

BORDER, BACKING & BINDING
- 1 yd coordinating fabric

SAMPLE QUILT
- **Hadley** by Denyse Schmidt for Free Spirit
- **Bella Solids Snow** (11) by Moda Fabrics

▸ *visit msqc.co/modblock for tutorials*
& info on how to make this quilt.

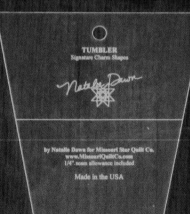

1 cut

Use the 5" *Tumbler Shape* from Missouri Star Quilt Co. to turn charm squares into tumblers. Find (2) 5" squares of the same print to pair up. Cut 17 pairs.

From the 5" solid squares, cut 70 tumbler shapes.

2 layout

Next, lay out the entire quilt center in an 8 x 13 setting. All tumblers lie on their sides. Start with a tumbler top facing toward the left. Match bottom to bottom **2A**, and top to top **2B** as you move across the row.

Begin with one row of solid tumblers. **2C** When adding print tumblers have the short top sides touch each other. Lay out your own bowtie design or follow the diagram. Don't be afraid to mix prints if you want.

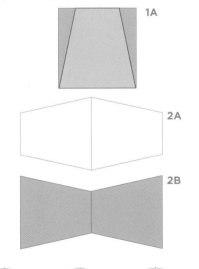

3 sew

Although the quilt was layed out in rows, it will be sewn together in columns. Starting at the upper left corner, sew a tumbler to the one directly below right sides together (RST). Offset the edges at the ¼" seam allowance making dog ears. Continue down the column. **3A**

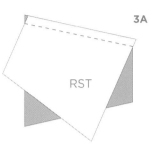

Press all seams in the first column down; all seams in the second column up and so on. **3B** Sew columns together nesting seams as you go. Press long column seams toward the center.

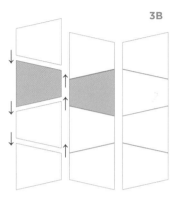

4 square up

Square up the zig-zaggy top and bottom edges. **4A** Depending on how much is trimmed, the quilt center now measures about . . .
Quilt center: 36½" x 47½"

5 borders

From the outer border fabric cut (5) 5" strips. Measure the width; cut top and bottom strips to that size and attach. Press to the borders. Repeat for both sides measuring the entire length; attach & press.

6 quilt & bind

Layer quilt top on batting and backing and quilt the way you like. Square up all raw edges.

Cut (6) 2½" strips from binding fabric to finish. For greater detail on finishing, check out the MSQC video tutorials. *See Supply List.*

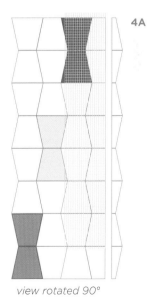

view rotated 90°

1 Use the MSQC 5" Tumbler Shape to cut the fabric squares. Step 1.

2 You will need a total of 34 (17 pairs) print and 70 solid tumblers.

3 Layout the entire quilt in columns first, placing the tumblers top-to-top to look like bowties. Step 2.

4 Tumblers are sewn together in columns first. Offset the 2 tumblers at the ¼" seam allowance, making dog ears. Step 3.

5 Next sew columns together lengthwise. A zig-zag edge at the top and bottom will be trimmed after the quilt center is together. Steps 3 & 4.

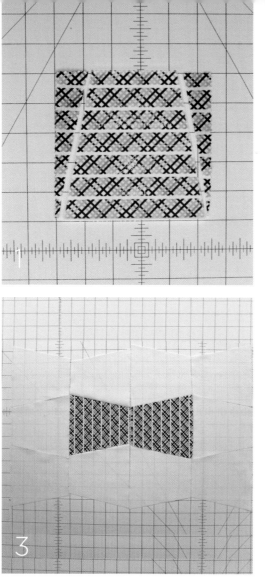
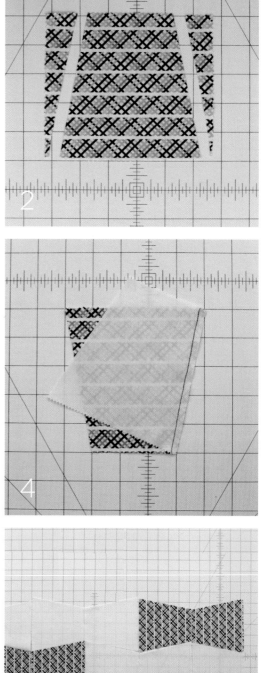

Bonus Pillow Project

1 cut

(2) print tumblers
(10) solid tumblers
(1) print 2" x 3" rect. from scrap
(2) 3" WOF strips &
(3) 2½" WOF strips from border,
     backing & binding fabric
½ yd muslin for quilting pillow top

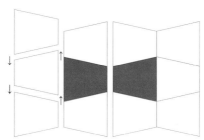

follow pressing arrows from column to column

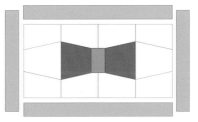

2 sew

Lay the tumblers out in a 3 x 4 setting with 2 "bowtie" tumblers positioned in the center. Sew the tumblers together in columns first; then sew the columns together. **2A**
(See Step 3 on page 41.)

Trim the zig-zag edges straight. Press the edges of the scrap rectangle under ¼." Position it between the print tumblers. Applique it to the pillow top by hand or machine.

Pillow center size: 18½" x 11"

3 borders

Subcut the 3" border into (2) 18½" long strips and attach them to the top and bottom edges. Press to the borders.

Then add (2) 16" strips to either side. Press to the borders. **3A**

4 finishing

Layer pillow top on batting and muslin. Quilt as desired. Square up. Cut backing to the same size as the pillow top. Layer them WST.

Sew the (3) 2½" binding strips together end-to-end using diagonal seams. Press seams open. Fold in half lengthwise. Press. Attach binding to the pillow top and back, leaving a 4" opening at the pillow's bottom edge. Stuff with fiberfill. Finish attaching the binding.

Turn the folded edge to the back and tack into place by hand.

Finished Pillow size: 24" x 16½"

continued from page 41: Enlarge a copy of this diagram. Outline the setting of the quilt size you want to make. Then color it in to create your own design.

Dapper Dan quilt

rainbow dreams
amy ellis

Half Square Triangles (HST) are incredibly versatile, both in design and in construction. They can be whipped up quickly to use in a variety of ways.

The challenge, though, is to make these triangles in the quantity needed for a whole quilt quickly and accurately. There are many techniques to create the HST. The obvious method is simply to sew two triangles together, but this usually ends up needing a lot of trimming. There are many shortcut alternatives. Our favorite method is to sandwich two squares and sew a ¼" all the way around the perimeter. Use your rotary cutter and a ruler and cut diagonally from point to point both ways and voilà! You have four HST ready to go!

We love this block because it comes together quickly and can create so many fun arrangements when combined in different ways. Try chopping them up again for totally different look. Depending on your color choice or layout you can quickly come up with lots of different designs. Make a zig-zag or a fun chevron using two complementary solids or use the Best. Day. Ever! fabric line like Amy did to create your own unique arrangement.

Playing with color can be so fun when working with HSTs. Depending on your palette or pattern choice you can create something new and creative. The possibilities are endless.

▶ leftovers are a good thing

Half square triangles are also a great way to use up leftover fabrics in your scrap bin. Keep a box of them trimmed to the same size. Once you have a bunch, start playing with different arrangements until you find a design you love. Any combination can make the cutest scrappy quilt!

squaring up

Having good tools that work well for you is important when squaring up HSTs. A sharp rotary blade and a rotating mat will save you time and save your wrists and back from needless pain.

▶ supply list

makes a 74½" X 80¾" quilt

QUILT TOP
- 1 print pack 10" squares
- 1 solid pack 10" squares

BINDING
- ¾ yd coordinating fabric

BACKING
- 5 yds 44" wide fabric
  OR 2½ yds 90" wide

TOOLS
- rotating cutting mat OR small
  cutting mat

SAMPLE QUILT
- **Best Day Ever!** by April Rosenthal
  for Moda Fabrics

- **Bella Solids White** (98) by Moda Fabrics

▶ *visit msqc.co/modblock for tutorials
& info on how to make this quilt.*

1 cut & select

Pair up each print square with a solid square RST (right sides together).

Sew a ¼″ around the perimeter of each pair pivoting at each corner.

Cut the pair in half 2X diagonally. A rotating cutting mat comes in handy at this point, or try a small mat that can be picked up and turned between cuts. Repeat for all pairs. Press seams to the print.

Block size: 6⅝″ x 6⅝″
Yield: (168)

Note: There will be more blocks than you need, but that will allow for a greater selection of color.

2 arrange

The key to this quilt is the colorful arrangement of the HSTs. Using a design wall, large table or floor space helps to arrange the blocks.

1 pair 1 solid & 1 print; stitch around the outside; cut 2 diagonals

2A color groups

blue   orange   yellow   multi
green   pink   white/nearly white

Stack blocks according to color. **2A**

Blocks are laid into a 12 x 13 grid. Begin at the top left-hand corner and work in columns. Build offset stripped pairs that slant one way in the even columns, and another way in the odd. Each slanted pair consists of 2 same-print HSTs. **2B**

Build each column following the color chart. Leave areas empty as shown in **2C**.

Next, construct the central hourglass block. Its upper left-hand corner is the 7th column over, 9th row down. **2D** Then build the outer square around it. **2E** Finish a partial square with the remaining blocks.

3 let's sew

Once you are pleased with the layout, begin sewing blocks together in rows first. Press seams in one direction on even rows; to the opposite direction in odd rows. Then sew rows together to build the quilt center.
Quilt Center Size: 74″ x 80″

4 quilt & bind

Layer quilt top on batting and backing and quilt the way you like. Square up all raw edges.

Cut (9) 2¼″ WOF strips from binding fabric to finish. For greater detail on finishing, check out the MSQC video tutorials. *See Supply List.*

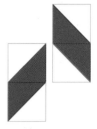

2B shown: 2 opposite stripped pairs offset

2C areas where the pattern of offset stripped pairs in columns repeats consistently

2D the central hourglass

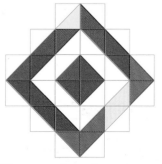

2E surrounding square around the hourglass

1 Pair up 1 solid & 1 print 10″ square right sides together (RST). Sew ¼″ around the perimeter. Step 1.

2 Without disturbing the fabric make 2 diagonal cuts across the pair. Yield: 4 half square triangles (HSTs). Step 1.

3 Press seams to the dark side.

4 Build offset stripped pairs that slant one way in the even columns and another way in the odd columns.

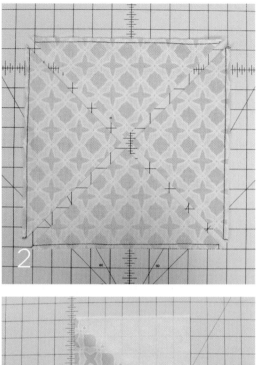

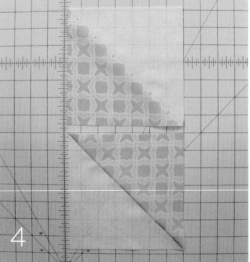

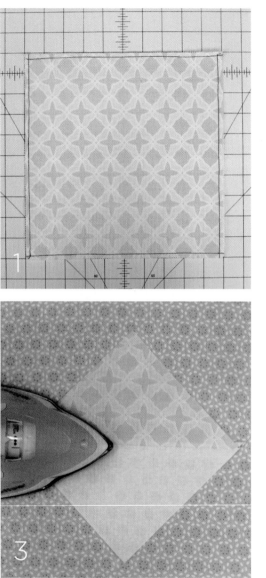

Copy and enlarge this diagram as often as you like. Color over the light grey triangles with colored pencils. Keep track of how many HSTs you have of each color print so that the design can be completed with the blocks you have.

▶ **TIP** *Be as creative as you'd like with the layout. You may want to focus on lighter colors for the center and move out to darker ones; or, have lighter HSTs in the upper left that fall to darker HSTs to the bottom right. Use the open chart above. Copy and enlarge it, then use colored pencils to audition your design.*

hexi gems
lisa hirsch

The Hexi Gem quilt is yet another great new way to use a our half hexagon tool. Lisa used a fusible applique technique to create a really beautiful gemstone star design. She says, "Being creative and artful is embedded into my everyday routine.

I love that I get to share techniques and the creative processes with my students." The half-hexies could be attached to the background squares using a variety of adhesives. Some of our favorites are fusible Heat 'n Bond, Lapel Stick, and applique glue. Once your hexies are attached and stitched down, you can be super creative with layout. Make a bunch of gems or just a few; this is your chance to take control of the design and create something one-of-a-kind!

The Hexi Gem pattern is the perfect showcase for a variety of different fabric lines and colors. The placement of your applique, your color choices, and how you combine them all lead to an amazingly customizable project that is unique every time. The basic idea of using a shape positioned strategically on a square and grouped together repeatedly could spark yet other fantastic quilts—the sky's the limit! Our hope is that Hexi Gem will inspire you to create many fun, new designs.

thread advice

Use a neutral thread color when applique piecing. Grey or beige are both commonly used. Thread doesn't have to be an exact match to your fabric but you'll want it to blend in so it doesn't call attention to itself.

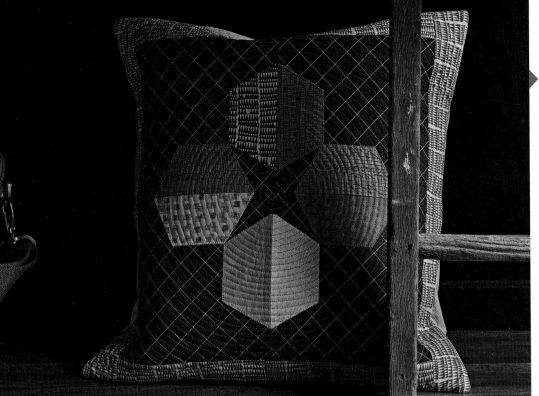

pillow talk

New to applique? That's ok! Try starting with a smaller project first, like a pillow. It's a great way to try something new without a huge time commitment or cost. Plus, if you like what you make you can decorate your home with it when you're finished!

fancy free, or not

Would you guess this quilt uses the same technique but in a different layout? The great thing about applique is that you can create whatever layout you want. Whether you're feeling carefree and organic or precise and structured, it doesn't matter because you're not held to any rules or block.

▸ supply list

makes a 58" X 67½" quilt

QUILT TOP
- 1 solid pack 10" squares
- 1 print pack 5" squares OR
  (22) 5" squares

BINDING
- ¾ yd coordinating fabric

BACKING
- 3¾ yds coordinating fabric

ADDITIONAL MATERIALS
- MSQC 5" half hexagon shape
- glue stick

SAMPLE QUILT
- **Doe** by Carolyn Friedlander
  for Robert Kaufman

- **Kona Cotton Coal** (1080)
  for Robert Kaufman

▸ *visit msqc.co/modblock for tutorials*
& info on how to make this quilt.

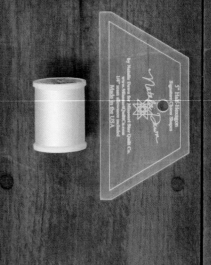

1 cut

From the (22) 5" print squares cut out 2 half-hexie shapes from each square with the MSQC Half-Hexagon shape. Lay the long bottom side along the precut's zig-zag edge, narrow top to the square's center. **1A** Or, cut the square in half, lining up the zig-zag edges and cut 2 half-hexies at a time. Throw all the half-hexies in a bag or basket and mix them up.

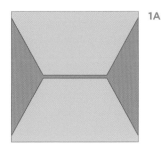

1A

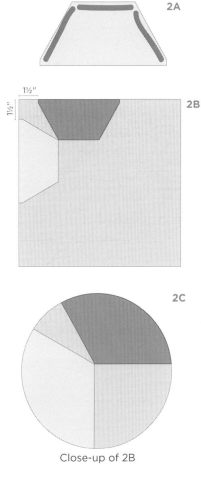

2A

1½"

2B

2C

Close-up of 2B

2 applique

Each "flower" will come together at the intersection of (4) 10" blocks. Each flower block will have 2 half-hexies positioned on either side of one corner.

Grab 2 half-hexies of different prints. Use a glue stick to apply glue to the side wrong side of the half-hexie along its sides & top. **2A** Position the long zig-zag bottoms on adjacent sides of the 10" square, 1½" down from a corner. **2B** The half-hexies should touch. **2C** (close-up) Press into place.

Set your machine to a buttonhole or narrow zig-zag stitch and secure the half hexies onto the square.

3 arrange & sew

Lay all the solid & appliqued blocks into a 6 x 7 setting. Wherever you want to position a "flower" select 4 of the appliqued blocks and face their hexies toward each other. **3A** There will also be a partial flower to position. Once you are satisfied with the block placement, begin sewing.

Starting in the upper left-hand corner, sew blocks together side-by-side to build rows. Press seams to one side in even rows; to the opposite side in odd rows.

Sew rows together, nesting the seams as you go. The zig-zag edges of the hexies have all disappeared into the quilt's seam allowances.

Quilt Center Size: 57½" x 67"

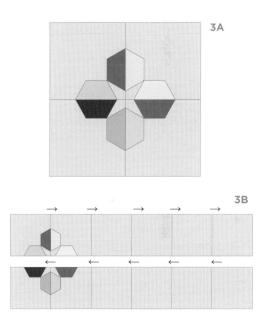

3A

3B

4 quilt & bind

Layer quilt top on batting and backing and quilt the way you like. Square up all raw edges.

Cut (7) 2½" strips from binding fabric to finish. For greater detail about finishing, check out the MSQC video tutorials. *See Supply List.*

1 Use the MSQC 5" Half Hexagon Shape to cut out fabric, 2 shapes from each 5" square. Here the square was cut in half first. Step 1.

2 You will need a total of 44 half-hexies. Step 1.

3 Applique the shapes to the fabric, long bottom edge matching the edge of a 10" square. There are several ways to adhere fabric: glue stick, Heat 'n Bond, or applique glue. Step 2.

4 The half-hexies sit on adjacent sides of a square—about 1½" down from the corner. They should touch each other at one point. Step 2.

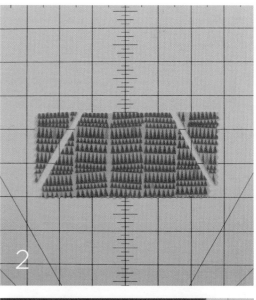

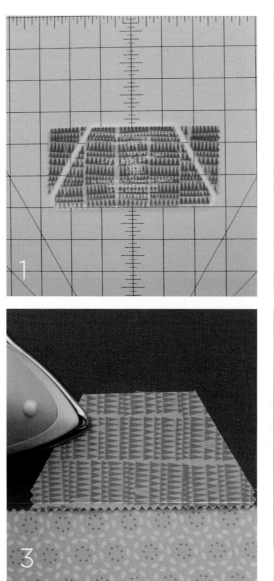

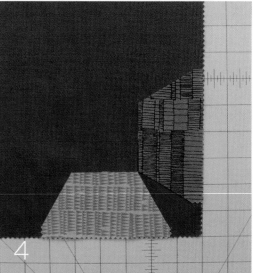

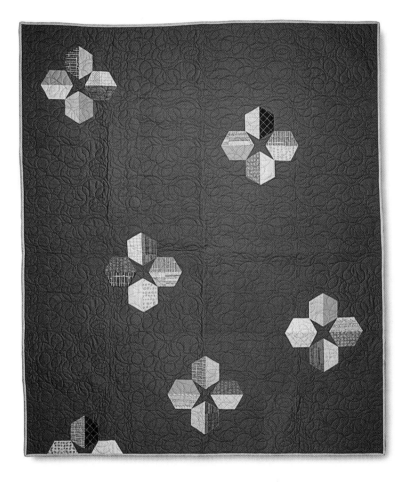

3C Photocopy and enlarge this diagram. Outline the setting of the size quilt you are making. Cut out the half hexie as a tracing template and use it to position flowers where you want them on the diagram. Use color pencils if you want.

noted
alexia abegg

This quilt is a classic and I'll tell you why. I walked into a local quilt shop and immediately recognized Noted draped over stacks of fabric bolts.

As I turned around, my eye caught sight of another version handing on the wall. It was totally different than the first. When I expressed my interest, the sales gal couldn't stop singing the praises of this quilt's design and how easily it came together.

At first glance it appears the envelopes are set on point, complete with set-in triangles and Y-seams. It looks so difficult to assemble. In actuality, the construction is much simpler and very straightforward. Think modified square-in-a-square with one side "mistakenly" flipped the wrong way.

What makes this a classic is the clever placement of those basic, time-tested half square triangles. Arranged so cleverly, the triangles completely morph into a modern day, fabric version of an Escher. Do you see the positive and negative envelopes, some open, some closed, some solid, some print? All of them are turned 45 degrees! And yet, I promise, these blocks were laid out in straight columns and rows. It's all perspective . . . and some genius construction.
Duly *Noted*!

▶ get creative

You can try low volume prints or play with a combination of solids and prints with this quilt. Whatever you choose, color is the key ingredient. This simple pattern design showcases your favorite prints in the very best way. Alexia chose to combine several of the Cotton + Steel fabric lines from their various collections and we love the result!

know your bias

Bias edges can be both friend and enemy. Take your time, pin at seam intersections, and try not to pull your fabric.

▸ supply list

makes a 62¼" X 86¾" quilt

QUILT TOP
- 1 pack 10" squares print
- 1 pack 10" squares solid OR
  2¾ yds solid yardage

BINDING
- ¾ yd coordinating fabric

BACKING
- 5¼ yds coordinating fabric

SAMPLE QUILT
- **Hatbox** by Alexia Macelle Abegg
  for Cotton + Steel

- **Basics Dottie Kerchief** (001)
  by Cotton + Steel

▸ *visit msqc.co/modblock for tutorials*
& info on how to make this quilt.

1 sew

If you chose to use solid yardage: Cut (9) 10" WOF strips; subcut into (36) 10" squares.

Pair (2) 10" squares right sides together (RST): (1) background solid & (1) print. **1A** Sew a ¼" seam around the entire outside edge.

You can stop and turn a quarter inch before the end or simply sew off the end—your choice. **1B**

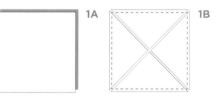

2 cut

Cut across the pair diagonally twice. A rotating cutting mat will help cut without moving the fabric.

Yield: 4 HSTs (half square triangles) Make 36 blocks. Keep same-print HSTs together. Do not press yet.

3 construct

Select 3 HSTs of the same print and 1 HST of another print to create an envelope. **3A** Press now according to the arrows for greater ease in nesting seams.

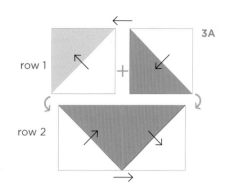

▶ **TIP** *nesting seams helps make more precise points.*

Join HSTs in rows together first. Press seams in each row in opposite directions. Sew the rows together nesting seams to make one envelope block. Press and square up to 12¾".

Block size: 12¾" x 12¾"
Yield: 36 blocks (35 required)

4 arrange & sew

Lay out blocks in an eye-pleasing fashion using a 5 x 7 setting. All the envelopes need to face the same direction. Try for an overall mix of light and dark values.

Now that the layout is determined, repress the horizontal seam of each block (if needed) so that they will nest from block to block across the row. See pressing arrows in **4A**.

Sew blocks into rows. Press all seams in even rows to the same side; all seams in odd rows to the opposite side. This practice will aid in nesting seams from row to row. Follow arrows in **4B**. Join rows to complete the quilt center.

Quilt center size: 61¾" x 86¼"

5 quilt & bind

Layer quilt top on batting and backing and quilt the way you like. Square up all raw edges.

Cut (8) 2½" strips from binding fabric to finish. For greater detail about finishing, check out the MSQC video tutorials. *See Supply List.*

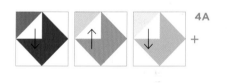

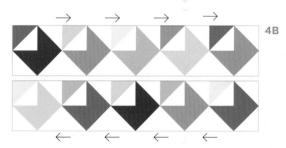

▶ **TIP** *make sure the envelopes are all facing the same direction.*

1 Pair up 1 solid & 1 print 10" square right sides together (RST). Sew ¼" around the perimeter. Step 1.

2 Without disturbing the fabric make 2 diagonal cuts across the pair. Yield: 4 half square triangles (HSTs). Step 1.

3 Use 3 HSTs of the same print turned toward each other and 1 HST of a different print. Position the last HST to look like an open envelope flap.

4 Now that you've made your selections, press the HSTs according to the pressing arrows in diagram 3B. This practice will help you nest seams together and result in more precise points.

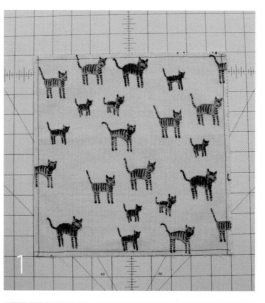
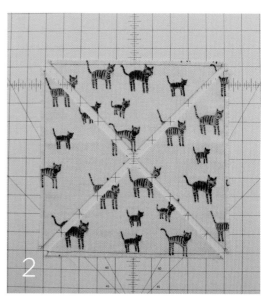
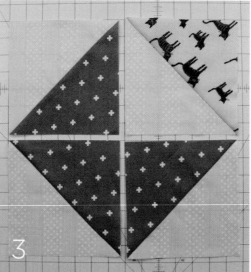
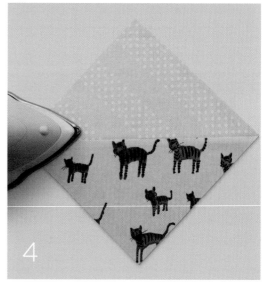

▸ improv tote
vanessa vargas wilson

This quilt-as-you-go tote bag is really fun to make! Vanessa introduced us to a great new product called Bosal Foam Interfacing. It gives you a really soft, yet sturdy foam lining for your projects that can be folded or crushed but always bounces back to the finished shape.

It is fusible on both sides but will only adhere to the side facing the iron which makes it really easy to use. This project gives you complete creative freedom as you decide where you start and what shape you use. Each time you change one of these design components, your finished piece changes, giving you a bag that is entirely unique every time!

Vanessa said, "I like to make a project like this in between big quilts to kinda give me a break. I like that it's just mindless piecing. No real measuring or precision patchwork. A quick tote project like that is good to break up the monotony of piecing tons of small pieces. It almost refreshes my mind while allowing me to use up scraps, or use a jelly roll where I really don't have to worry about fabrics matching since they will all go perfectly together."

Plus, you might just fall in love with fusible foam. A simple tap of the iron holds fabric in place. It's almost like having another pair of hands to help you work. If you've never tried a quilt-as-you-go project, this is the perfect place to start!

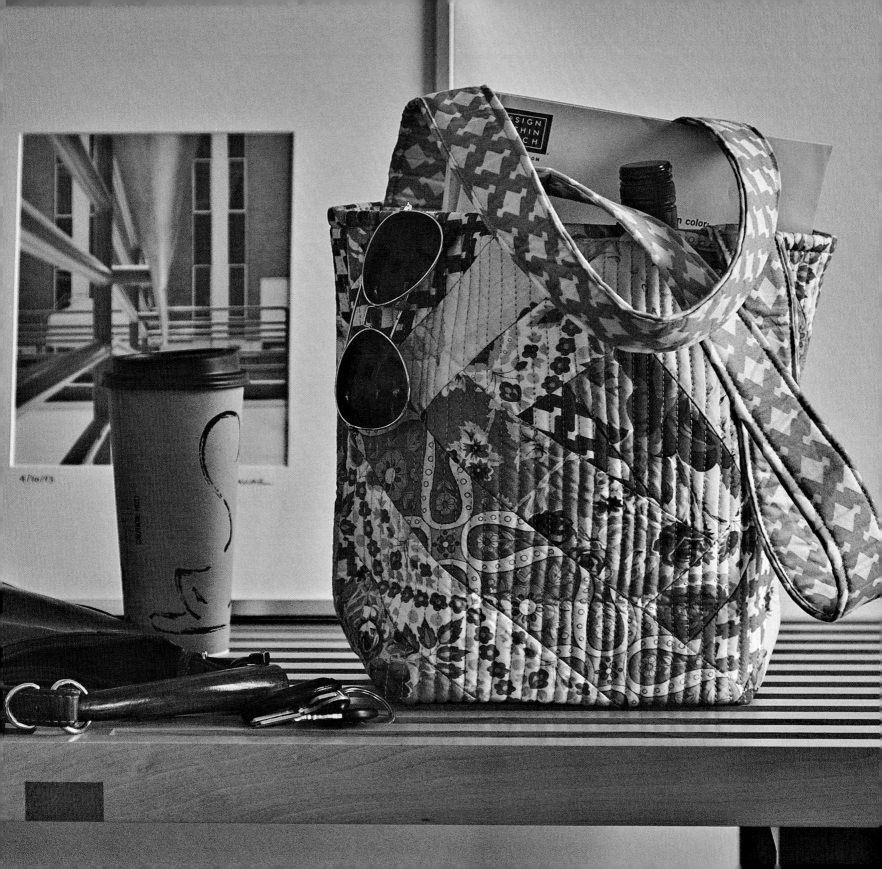

easy peasy

Why do we love quilt-as-you-go projects? Easy . . . when you're done piecing, so is your quilt, or bag as the case may be. Additional quilting is optional, not necessary!

▸ supply list

Makes a 12″ X 28″ tote

TOTE MATERIALS
- (1) 2½″ WOF roll print strips
- 1 yd coordinating fabric for lining
  & shoulder straps

OTHER SUPPLIES
- (1) package 18″ x 58″ Bosal's
  In-R-Form Plus foam interfacing

SAMPLE QUILT
- **Good Company** by Jennifer
  Paganelli for Free Spirit Fabric

▸ *visit msqc.co/modblock for tutorials & info on how to make this tote.*

1 create the fabric

Begin by cutting (2) 1½″ x 58″ strips from the length of the foam interfacing. Shorten them to 36″ and set aside for shoulder straps. **1A**

Cut the remaining foam into a 15″ x 30″ rectangle for the main body of the bag. **1A**

The piecing technique employed is free form. It is best to cut fabric strips as needed.

From a 2½″ strip, cut a square, rectangle, triangle or any straight-sided shape the size you want. **1B** Place the piece on the foam. How straight or offset this first piece is placed will determine how abstract the piecing design will be—the more offset, the more abstract. **1C**

Choose one side of the first piece and cut another piece of fabric to that length. Lay the second piece RST on the first and stitch them together through the 2 layers of fabric and the foam interfacing. **1D**

2 tacking by iron

Using only the tip of the iron, tack the fabric open to expose the right sides of both pieces. Careful not to touch the iron to the exposed fusible on the foam.

Continue adding random fabric pieces in this fashion cutting lengths to the size of any side of the patchwork.

When the entire foam rectangle is covered in fabric, give your patchwork a good press to fuse the fabrics to the foam. **2A** If you want to do any additional quilting now is the time to do so.

Flip the foam/fabric rectangle to the back side and trim away excess fabric. **2B**

3 bag shape

Fold the rectangle in half, fabric to the inside and short sides matching (bag top). Sew a ½″ seam down both sides toward the fold, backstitching at the beginning and end. **3A**

At the folded end of the bag, pinch the corners flat, creating a triangle with the bag's seam running down the middle of it. Measure 2½″ from the tip of the triangle. Draw a line perpendicular across the bag's seam. **3B** Pin in place. Sew

(2x) 1½″ x 36″ — 1A

15″ x 30″

1B

1C

2 examples of starting the fabric

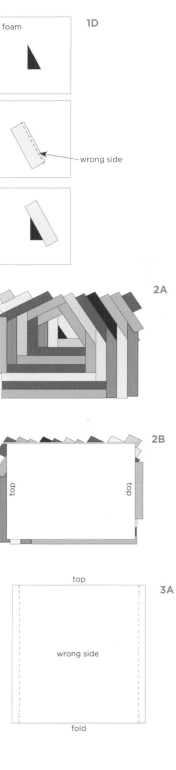

foam — 1D

wrong side

2A

2B

top

top

top — 3A

wrong side

fold

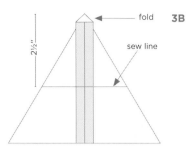

3B

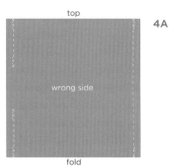

4A

4B

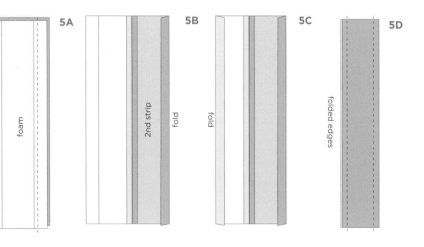

5A　**5B**　**5C**　**5D**

on the drawn line backstitching at both ends. Either trim away excess or leave the triangle portion in place for added weight & support of the bag's bottom. Repeat for the other corner of the bag's bottom. Turn the bag right side out.

4 lining

From the lining fabric cut a 15" WOF strip; remove selvages. Subcut the strip into (1) 30" long rectangle. Repeat step 3 above but leave a 3"-4" opening in the middle of one side seam (backstitching at the opening's ends). **4A**

Sew across the corners of the lining as well. Trim triangle corners to ½." **4B** Do *not* turn right side out.

5 straps

Cut (4) 2½" WOF strips from the lining/strap fabric; subcut them to 36" long.

At the ironing board lay a 2½" fabric strip on top of a 1½" x 36" foam strip right side facing up and centering it as best as possible. Fuse the fabric onto the foam strip.

Using a second 2½" strip of fabric *(shown as green for demonstration purposes)* RST to the first, sew the 2 strips together along one long side only. Use a seam allowance that gets you close to the foam without actually sewing on it, about ¼"–⅜" works well. **5A**

Work with the strap so that the foam is exposed and the right side of the fabric is facing down. Fold the other long side of the second strip in about ½" to ¾" and press to finish that edge. **5B**

Fold up the first strip of fabric (light blue here) on the side of the foam that does not have the seam. **5C** Tack into place with the tip of the iron.

Bring the fold of the second strip *(green)* over the foam to encase all raw edges entirely. Fuse into place. Pin the 2 folded edges together and topstitch along both long sides of the strap to finish. **5D** Make 2 straps.

6 assembly

Cut the straps to the length you'd like plus ¾." With one side of the outer bag facing, measure 4" in from both side seams and place the strap ends into position matching raw edges to the

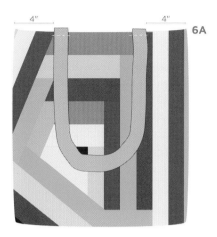

6A

4" 4"

bag's raw edge. Careful not to twist the straps. **6A** Sew the strap to the outer bag ¼" from the top. Repeat on the other side with the second strap.

Slip the outer bag into the lining RST. Make sure the straps are lying down between the lining and the outer bag. Match raw edges at the top and match side seam to side seam of the lining and outer bag. Pin together along the top raw edge.

Stitch around the top of the bag with a ½" seam allowance. **6B**

6B

opening

Flip the entire bag right side out through the opening of the lining. Press the lining. Machine or hand stitch the opening shut.

Then tuck the lining back into the bag, rolling it away from the top edge so that it does not show to the right side. Tack it into position by pressing along the top edge.

Topstitch along the top edge. **6C** Finished!

6C

▶ **TIP** *Try topstitching with decorative stitches. Nothing shouts "one-of-a-kind" like a custom touch!*

double friendship star
jenny doan

Using contrasting colors in a quilt helps to add visual interest and dimension. The Double Friendship Star can be a fun lesson in color selection.

When you use two contrasting colors the friendship stars are so easy to see. Without contrasting colors, you may lose the star pattern all together.

This contrast effect can be achieved in a couple of ways. One way is to use complementary colors like a blue and yellow, or a purple and green combination. Or, you can go with color value. Choose a dark and a light of the same color to create the contrast. Sometimes it can be hard to see value and contrast so we have a couple of fun tricks to help you out.

One of the easiest ways to see contrast is to use the Sew Red Glasses or a red transparent filter. Another handy trick is to take a picture using either a phone or camera. Then render the photo black and white, removing all color as an easy way to see contrast and value better. Whichever method you use, the Double Friendship Star is a wonderful design to try out your favorites on the color wheel and make them pop.

▶ scrap salvage

You will have a stack of triangles leftover after making this quilt. But instead of waste, make table runners! Stitch together pinwheels or zig-zags, hearts or hourglasses. Just create!

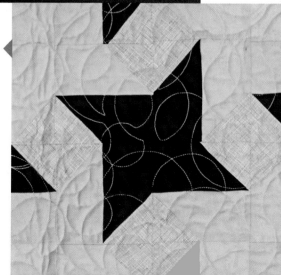

press, do not push ◄

Pressing the seam of 2 strips sewn together lengthwise can be tricky. To prevent "arcing" do not push the top fabric back aggressively with the iron. Instead, set the seam, open the top strip and lift the iron up & down to press.

▸ supply list

makes a 49" X 57" quilt

QUILT TOP
for star A (primary) & star B (secondary) each:
- (1) 2½" WOF half-roll (20 count) OR 1½ yds contrasting fabric
- 1¾ yds solid background yardage

BINDING
- ½ yd coordinating fabric

BACKING
- 3¼ yds coordinating fabric

SAMPLE QUILT
- **Bella Solids Navy** (20) **& Sky** (177) by Moda Fabrics

- **Architextures Curry** (291) by Carolyn Friedlander for Robert Kaufman

- **Basics XO Night Owl** (006) by Cotton + Steel for RJR

▸ *visit msqc.co/modblock for tutorials & info on how to make this quilt.*

1 cut & sew

From the background fabric, cut (22) 2½" WOF strips; subcut into 2½" squares. Set aside.

Total req'd: (336) 2½" squares

Cut star solid A & B fabrics into (19) 2½" WOF strips each.

Sew (1) star A and (1) star B strips together lengthwise. **1A** Press to the dark side. Make (19) strip sets.

Subcut the strip sets into 4½" squares. Stack them uniformly; for example, all star A strips on the bottom. **1B**

Yield: (9) 4½" squares per strip set
Total req'd: (168) blocks

2 build the block

Iron a diagonal crease into each of the 2½" background squares. This will be the sewing line.

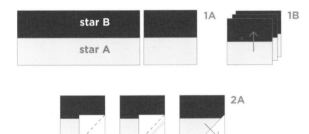

▶ **TIP** *the crease in the 2½" background square should connect 2 sides of the block.*

Position the background square on a corner. Sew across, trim away excess. Follow pressing arrows. **2A** Chain piecing will speed up this step. **2B** The 2½" square must be in the same position on every block. All blocks will be identical.

Set another square on the opposite corner. **2C**

Use (4) 4½" blocks. Arrange them so that the star A color is joined in the center (primary star). **2D** Like a 4-patch, sew blocks together in rows; then the rows to each other. Repeat for all blocks. Consistency is important.

Yield: (42) 8½" identical blocks

3 arrange center

Lay the blocks in a 6 x 7 setting. Note the secondary friendship star appearing. Sew blocks together in rows first. Press seams to one side in even rows; to the opposite side in odd rows. Then sew rows together to make the quilt center. **3A**

Quilt Center size: 48½" x 56½"

4 quilt & bind

Layer quilt top on batting and backing and quilt the way you like. Square up all raw edges.

Cut (7) 2½" strips from binding fabric to finish. For greater detail about finishing, check out the MSQC video tutorials. *See Supply List.*

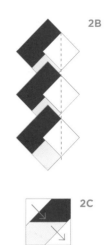

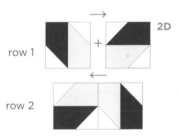

▶ **TIP** *the pressing arrows offer the best option for nesting seams in the next step.*

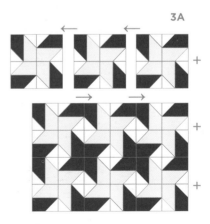

1 Sew 2 strips of star fabric A & B together. Press and cut into 4½″ squares. Yield: 9 squares per strip set. Step 1.

2 Snowball 2 opposite corners of the block by placing 2½″ squares on the corners and sewing across. Step 2.

3 Consistency is VERY important. The same corners are snowballed on every block. Yield: ¼ block. Step 2.

4 Use (4) 4½″ snowballed blocks. Turn the primary color (A fabric) to the center to form a friendship star. The secondary stars will form when the rows and columns of the quilt are constructed. Step 2.

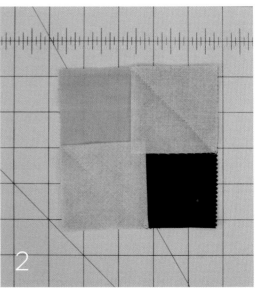

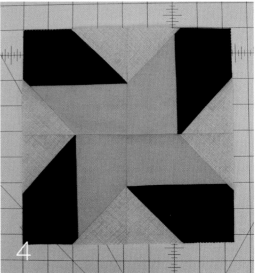

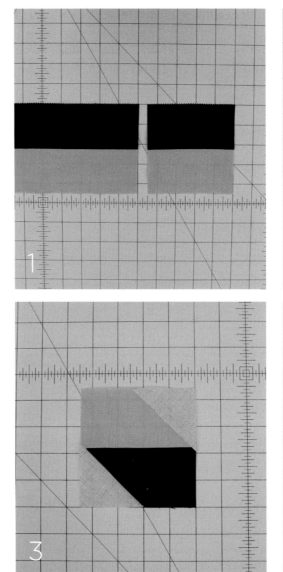

4 The primary color (A fabric), in this case light blue, will appear as complete stars; the secondary star (B fabric), here the dark blue, will have partial stars around the perimeter of the quilt.

stardust
amy ellis

The classic periwinkle quilt was originally pieced by hand from small carefully cut scraps of fabric. That all changed when an antique quilt landed in the hands of Jenny Doan.

Jenny, Natalie and MSQC developed triangle papers and an acrylic template to make the periwinkle block a far simpler endeavor. Now Amy has come up with a further evolution of the block. Instead of combining 4 triangles to form a periwinkle, she uses only two. This immediately sets the block on an angle. Plus, her selection of light neutral fabrics for the "kite" surrounded by matching prints gives the former periwinkle a definitive modern take.

Without modern paper piecing techniques, this quilt would be a daunting undertaking. And if you've never tried paper piecing this is the opportunity to jump in. Developed as a way to construct complex blocks with small pieces more easily, you may be delighted to experience greater accuracy and speed when using this technique.

The idea is to cover a paper template with fabric by sewing right through the paper and fabric alike; then use the template as a cutting guide. The stitches perforate the paper making it easy to tear it away. We think you'll fall for paper piecing once you've tried these wonderful tools.

▶ mark it up

Here's a shortcut: instead of cutting out each shape, you can use a fabric marking pen to trace the long edges of the Mini Wacky Web Shape onto 2½" squares. Then align the rectangles to the drawn line. Trim excess fabric after removing the paper.

tools of the trade

While trimming your triangle units, make
sure you are prepared. Having all the tools you need
at hand (including a trash bin) makes for a much
smoother and neater process. For the best scrappy
look, use a design wall or the floor to layout the quilt.
Aim for lots of movement and subtle shifts in color.
Then stitch the rows together.

▶ supply list

makes a 46½" X 53½" quilt

QUILT TOP
- 2 print jelly rolls
- (4) ½ yd cuts of coordinating light fabric

BINDING
- ½ yd coordinating fabric

BACKING
- 3 yds coordinating fabric

ADDITIONAL TOOLS
- Mini Wacky Web Shape
- 2 packets of Triangle papers, small
- glue stick

SAMPLE QUILT
- **Persimmon** by BasicGrey for Moda Fabrics
- **Grunge** by BasicGrey for Moda Fabrics

▶ *visit msqc.co/modblock for tutorials & info on how to make this quilt.*

1 cut

From the (4) light half yard fabrics, cut (6) 2½" WOF strips from each (24 WOF strips total). Then use the Mini Wacky Web Shape from MSQC to cut "kites," 16 per strip. Cut an additional 2 kites each from 3 light fabrics.

Total: 390 kites.

From the 2½" print strips select 65 of the dark to medium fabrics. Cut them into (12) 3½" rectangles each. Stack according to print.

Total: (780) 2½" x 3½" rectangles

2 construct

Glue one kite right side facing up to a piece of triangle paper. The top of the kite should fit into the 90° corner of the paper triangle. Just use a dab of glue. Too much and the paper will be difficult to remove.

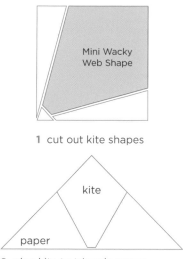

1 cut out kite shapes

2 glue kite to triangle paper

3 sew

Attach a 3½" print rectangle to one side of the kite RST. Sew right through the paper with a ¼" seam allowance. Finger press open. The fabric should cover one leg of the paper triangle. Repeat for the other leg of the triangle using the same print. **3A & B** Press open. **3C** Repeat for all the kites.

4 trim

Flip the kite unit over and trim excess fabric using the triangle paper as a pattern. At this point remove the paper backing. It should tear easily along the stitching lines.

5 block

Sew the longest side of 2 kite units together, matching kite tails in the middle. Pin and sew RST.

Block size: 4" x 4" squared up
Total: 195

6 layout & sew

Lay out the blocks in a 13 x 15 grid mixing colors in an eye-pleasing fashion. Start with a kite pointing up to the left. As you lay each block in, turn kites so their "heads" meet from block to block across and from row to row down.

Sew blocks together across to build rows; then rows together to complete quilt center. Nest seams.

Quilt Center Size: 46" x 53"

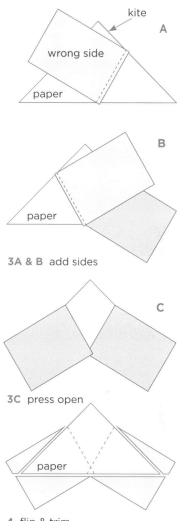

3A & B add sides

3C press open

4 flip & trim

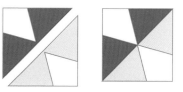

5 sew 2 triangles together to make a block; kite tails point toward each other; square up to 4"

1. Use the MSQC Mini Wacky Web Shape to cut fabric. Step 1.

2. For this quilt you will need 390 "kite" shapes cut.

3. Use a sparse amount of glue to tack the kite to the triangle paper. Note how the kite's top point fits perfectly in the triangle's 90 degree corner. Step 2.

4. Sew a rectangle to one side of the kite shape. Press open and repeat for the other side. Step 3.

5. Flip the triangle over. With a rotary cutter and ruler cut off excess fabric around the triangle paper. Remove paper by tearing it away from the stitched lines. Step 4.

6. Sew 2 triangle blocks together along their bottom edges to form a square. The kite tails will face each other. Note that this sample is yet another color variation of the block. Step 5.

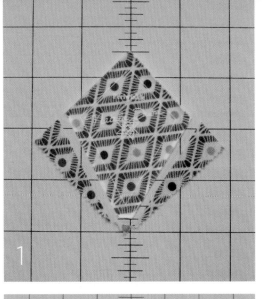

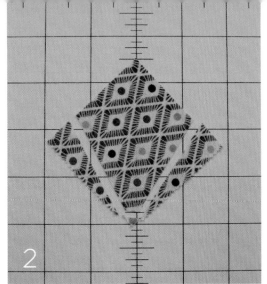

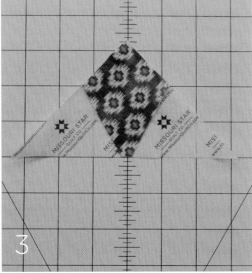

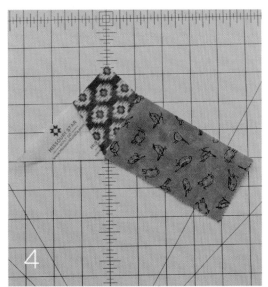

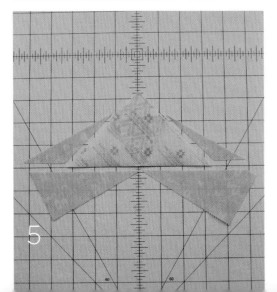

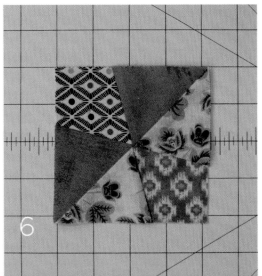

7 quilt & bind

Layer quilt top on batting and backing and quilt the way you like. Square up all raw edges.

Cut (6) 2¼" strips from binding fabric to finish. For greater detail about finishing, check out the MSQC video tutorials. *See Supply List.*

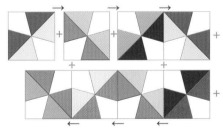

6 turn the heads of the kites to meet each other from block to block and from row to row

confetti
jenny doan

We have been seeing ombré (pronounced AHM-brey) in fashion and clothing for some time now. It's even begun showing up in the quilting world, and the effects are amazing!

This lovely term for a simple tone-on-tone gradient is not only fun to say but more fun to make in a quilt. Our Small Simple Wedge tool is the star of this ombré show, making the color a playful arrangement of interesting shapes as it moves from light to dark. It reminds us of a beautiful Italian mosaic or confetti collage. A simple trend and MSQC's great tools created a beautiful and stunning design. You can too!

It's helpful when doing an ombré to have several colored fabrics in various shades to give you the right effect. Start with a light, medium, and dark tone-on-tone color range. Then begin to add other light and medium values into the mix until you feel like you have enough to create the effect you want.

To arrange Jenny's triangle quilt, she used 7-10 different shades of colors from the Pretty Peonies fat quarter bundle. Using this bundle took the work out of gathering fabrics and picking colors. But, regardless of which approach you take to choose your colors and shades, utilizing this simple technique will give you a beautiful quilt design that will have your friends talking!

play with color

Be creative when you
layout this quilt! There
are so many options
when playing with color
placement. You can make a
new design just by the way
things are arranged—make
it your own.

to blend or not to blend, that is the question

Remember that the fabrics you choose determine the starting points of dark and light. For example, put medium blue next to a light fabric and it's a dark. Sew the same medium blue fabric to a black fabric and it becomes a medium.

▶ supply list

makes a 53" X 73" quilt

QUILT TOP
• (1) fat quarter pack of 22 fabrics

BINDING
• ⅝ yd coordinating fabric

BACKING
• 3½ yds coordinating fabric

ADDITIONAL TOOLS
• MSQC Small Triangle Shape

SAMPLE QUILT
• Pretty Peonies by Robert
  Kaufman

▶ *visit msqc.co/modblock for tutorials*
& info on how to make this quilt.

1 cut

Organize the fat quarters (FQs) in 3 groups of 7-8 each, either by value (light, medium, dark), or color (blue, green, yellow, for example). It will depend on the FQ collection.

Remove the selvage of each FQ. From this edge, cut (4) 4½" WOF strips—approx. 21" long. Use the *MSQC Small Simple Wedge* and cut 10-14 triangles from each strip. **1A** Flip the shape up and down cutting the angled sides as you move across the strip. Depending on the usable fabric in each FQ you will have 40-48 triangles.

2 begin sewing

Start with one group. Sew triangles together randomly in pairs side-to-side. Match the top of one triangle to the bottom of the other. Offset the edges, creating dog ears at the beginning and end of the ¼" seam allowance. **2A**

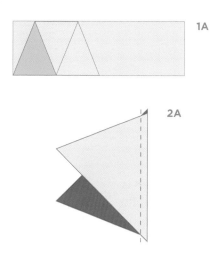

1A

2A

▶ **TIP** *An alternate method of pressing when working with difficult shapes is to press all seams open and use pins to align points through the fabric layers.*

Chain piece. Make 130 pairs from this group. The remaining triangles are unpaired stragglers. These will come in handy later.

Combine the pairs into sets of 4. Before sewing, press or repress the seams in the set to face the same direction; sew the pairs together. Press the last seam in the same direction. **2B** Make 60 sets of 4.

Repeat for the other 2 color/value groups.

3 arrange

Lay out the triangle sets from one value/color group into 15 columns. The column lengths can vary a bit at this point. Here's where the stragglers come in. Wherever you need extra pairs or a single triangle, select from the collection of leftovers. Mixing stragglers in from other groups will create a sense of overlap and flow from one value/color to the next. Experiment to get the look you are after. Extend the columns with sets from the other 2 color/value groups, blending colors as you go.

General layout guidelines:

• All seams within a column should lay in the same direction. Turn the sets when necessary. **3A**

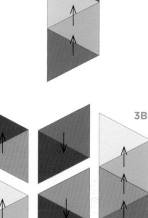

3A

3B

• From column to column triangles butt up bottom to bottom & top to top. **3A**

• The final count will be 55 triangles per column.

4 build the center

Sew sets, pairs and single triangles together columnwise according to your layout. Press seams in the same direction of others in its column.

Then sew columns together matching points at each juncture. Nest seams whenever possible between columns, and use pins to line up points before

1 Flip the MSQC Small Triangle Shape up and down across the fabric strip to cut out the shapes. Step 1.

2 After sorting fabrics according to value or color pair up triangles of one color/value group and sew together. Note that 1 triangle is upside down as you sew them RST along their sides. Step 2.

3 Sew only a portion of the pairs into sets of 4 (about 60). The stragglers will be used later to create the shading effect. Step 2.

4 Triangles will face each other top-to-top and bottom-to-bottom from column to column. Step 3.

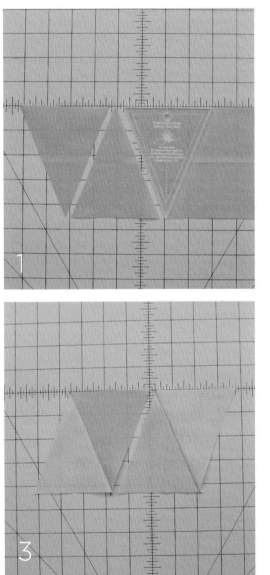

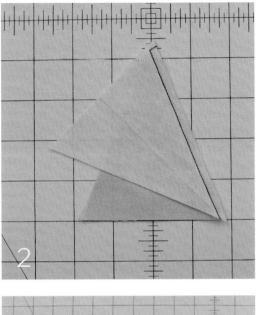

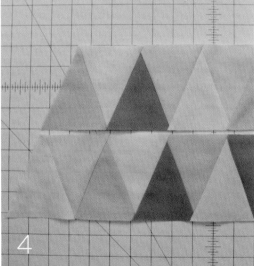

sewing seams. To reduce bulk press these final seams open.

Square up the top and bottom zig-zaggy edges.

Quilt Center Size: 52½" x 73½"

5 quilt & bind

Layer quilt top on batting and backing and quilt the way you like. Square up all raw edges.

Cut (7) 2½" strips from binding fabric to finish. For greater detail about finishing, check out the MSQC video tutorials. *See Supply List.*

Broken Bars 67½" X 91"

Designed/Shea Henderson Pieced/Kelly McKenzie
Quilted/Cassie Martin

QUILT TOP
- (1) 22-24 fat quarter bundle

BINDING
- ¾ yd coordinating fabric

BACKING
- 5½ yds coordinating fabric

SAMPLE QUILT
- Shaman by Parson Gray for Free Spirit (warm colorway)
- Patchwork City by Elizabeth Hartman for Robert Kaufman (cool colorway)

QUILTING PATTERN
- Square Meander

Confetti Quilt 53" X 73"

Designed/Jenny Doan Pieced/Natalie Earnheart
Quilted/Sherry Melton

QUILT TOP
- (1) fat quarter pack of 22 fabrics

BINDING
- ⅝ yd coordinating fabric

BACKING
- 3½ yds coordinating fabric

ADDITIONAL TOOLS
- MSQC Small Triangle Shape

SAMPLE QUILT
- Pretty Peonies by Robert Kaufman

QUILTING PATTERN
- Simple Stipple

Dapper Dan 46" X 56½"

Designed/Natalie Earnheart Pieced/Kelly McKenzie
Quilted/Amber Weeks

QUILT TOP
- 2 packs 5" solid squares
- 1 pack 5" print squares
- ¾ yd outer border fabric

BINDING
- ½ yd coordinating fabric

BACKING
- 3 yds coordinating fabric

ADDITIONAL MATERIALS
- MSQC 5" Tumbler Shape

QUILTING PATTERN
- Loops & Swirls

PILLOW TOP
- (10) 5" solid leftover squares
- (2) 5" print leftover squares
- 2" x 3" contrasting scrap
- fiberfill stuffing

BORDER, BACKING & BINDING
- 1 yd coordinating fabric

SAMPLE QUILT
- Hadley by Denyse Schmidt for Free Spirit
- Bella Solids Snow (11) by Moda Fabrics

Double Friendship Star 49" X 57"

Designed/Jenny Doan Pieced/Natalie Earnheart
Quilted/Emma Jensen

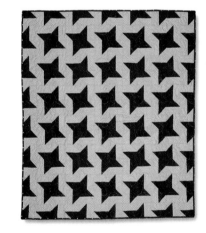

QUILT TOP *for star A (primary) & star B (secondary) each:*
- (1) 2½" WOF half-roll (20 count) OR 1½ yds contrasting fabric
- 1¾ yds solid background yardage

BINDING
- ½ yd coordinating fabric

BACKING
- 3¼ yds coordinating fabric

SAMPLE QUILT
- Bella Solids Navy (20) & Sky (177) by Moda Fabrics
- Architextures Curry (291) by Carolyn Friedlander for Robert Kaufman
- Basics XO Night Owl (006) by Cotton + Steel for RJR

QUILTING PATTERN
- Arc Doodle

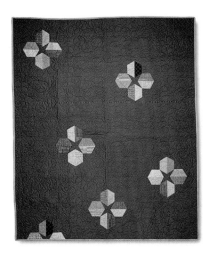

Hexi Gems 58" X 67½"

Designed/Pieced/Lisa Hirsch Quilted/Amber Weeks

QUILT TOP
- 1 solid pack 10" squares
- 1 print pack 5" squares OR (22) 5" squares

BINDING
- ¾ yd coordinating fabric

BACKING
- 3¾ yds coordinating fabric

ADDITIONAL MATERIALS
- MSQC 5" half hexagon shape
- glue stick

SAMPLE QUILT
- Doe by Carolyn Friedlander for Robert Kaufman
- Kona Cotton Coal (1080) for Robert Kaufman

QUILTING PATTERN
- Arc Doodle

Noted 62¼" X 86¾"

Designed/Pieced/Alexia Abegg Quilted/Jamey Stone

QUILT TOP
- 1 pack 10" squares print
- 1 pack 10" squares solid OR 2¾ yds solid yardage

BINDING
- ¾ yd coordinating fabric

BACKING
- 5¼ yds coordinating fabric

SAMPLE QUILT
- Hatbox by Alexia Macelle Abegg for Cotton + Steel
- Basics Dottie Kerchief (001) by Cotton + Steel

QUILTING PATTERN
- Arc Doodle

Rainbow Dreams 74½" X 80¾"

Designed/Pieced/Amy Ellis Quilted/Amber Weeks

QUILT TOP
- 1 print pack 10" squares
- 1 solid pack 10" squares

BINDING
- ¾ yd coordinating fabric

BACKING
- 5 yds 44" wide fabric
  OR 2½ yds 90" wide

TOOLS
- rotating cutting mat OR small
  cutting mat

SAMPLE QUILT
- Best Day Ever! by April
  Rosenthal for Moda Fabrics

- Bella Solids White (98) by
  Moda Fabrics

QUILTING PATTERN
- Jills Bubbles

River Log Cabin 65" X 81"

Designed/Pieced/Amy Ellis Quilted/Mari Zullig

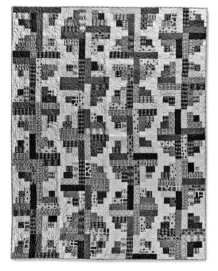

QUILT TOP
- (2) 2½" WOF rolls print
- 1¾ yds background solid OR (1) 1½" WOF roll background solid

BINDING
- ¾ yd coordinating fabric

BACKING
- 5 yds OR 2 yds 90" wide

SAMPLE QUILT
- Modern Neutrals by Amy Ellis for Moda Fabrics
- Bella Solids Eggshell (281) by Moda Fabrics

QUILTING PATTERN
- Champagne Bubbles

Stardust 46½" X 53½"

Designed/Pieced/Amy Ellis Quilted/Sherry Melton

QUILT TOP
• 2 print jelly rolls
• (4) ½ yd cuts of coordinating light fabric

BINDING
• ½ yd coordinating fabric

BACKING
• 3 yds coordinating fabric

ADDITIONAL TOOLS
• Mini Wacky Web Shape
• 2 packets of Triangle papers, small
• glue stick

SAMPLE QUILT
• Persimmon by BasicGrey for Moda Fabrics
• Grunge by BasicGrey for Moda Fabrics

Improv Tote 12" X 28"

Designed/Pieced/Quilted/Vanessa Vargas Wilson

TOTE MATERIALS
• (1) 2½" WOF roll print strips
• 1 yd coordinating fabric for lining & shoulder straps

OTHER SUPPLIES
• (1) package 18" x 58" Bosal's In-R-Form Plus foam interfacing

SAMPLE BAG
• Good Company by Jennifer Paganelli for Free Spirit Fabrics